Atul's Sacrifice:
The Heroic Struggle Against False 498a and other Cases

Save Indian Family Foundation

Published by Rajeev Lochan and Joy Bose

Contents

Dedication

This book is dedicated to all the men in India who are trapped in false court cases related to matrimonial disputes. Most of all, this is dedicated to Atul Subhash, a bright son of India who tragically gave up his life on the 9th of December 2024 in protest against the biased laws.

Preface

This book is a tribute to **Atul Subhash**, a brave and tormented soul who became a victim of one of the greatest injustices of our time—the misuse of matrimonial and family laws in India. Atul's tragic story is not an isolated incident but a reflection of a growing epidemic where biased laws and systemic corruption conspire to ruin lives, alienate fathers, and destroy families. His heroic sacrifice stands as a stark reminder of the human cost of a deeply flawed legal system.

As members of the **Save Indian Family Foundation (SIFF)**, India's largest NGO fighting against the misuse of laws like Section 498A, Domestic Violence Act, and CrPC 125, we dedicate this book to Atul and the countless other men who have suffered silently under the weight of false accusations. Our mission is to advocate for fairness, equity, and justice for men trapped in a legal system that often presumes their guilt and denies them the benefit of doubt.

The Story of a Broken System

Atul's story is emblematic of how laws originally designed to protect can be weaponized to exploit. Section 498A, hailed as a shield for women against dowry harassment, has evolved into a tool of extortion in many cases. Courts are flooded with false allegations, clogging the judicial system, tarnishing reputations, and destroying families. Meanwhile, genuine victims—both men and women—are left without recourse, their cries for justice drowned in a sea of misuse.

Atul's experiences shed light on:

- The harassment of men and their families through baseless accusations.

- The corruption within the judiciary, where bribes often dictate the outcome of cases.

- The alienation of fathers from their children, turning parental love into a weapon for financial and emotional blackmail.

- The stigma and isolation faced by men accused under these laws, often leading to mental health struggles, financial ruin, and, in tragic cases, suicide.

Atul's Heroic Sacrifice

Through his suicide note, Atul did not just recount his own suffering but left behind a call to action for society. His death was not an act of despair alone—it was a courageous attempt to expose the systemic rot in our legal system and the devastating consequences of legal misuse. His words resonate with the anguish of thousands of men who endure similar fates, and his story serves as a rallying cry for change.

A Call for Reform

This book is not merely an account of Atul's life and struggles but also a demand for reform. It is a plea to policymakers, the judiciary, and society at large to:

- Recognize the misuse of matrimonial laws and address it through legislative and judicial safeguards.

- Implement gender-neutral laws to ensure fairness for all.

- Introduce strict penalties for false accusations to deter misuse.

- Provide psychological and legal support for men who are victims of harassment.

A Movement for Justice

As SIFF members, we have seen firsthand the pain and suffering inflicted by these biased systems. Our mission is to fight for justice, provide support to those in distress, and advocate for a society where laws protect the innocent rather than empower the manipulative. Atul's story is not just his own—it is the story of every man wrongfully accused, every father alienated from his child, and every family torn apart by false allegations.

Through this book, we hope to honour Atul's memory and ensure that his death was not in vain. We aim to ignite conversations, challenge biases, and push for meaningful change in our legal and societal frameworks. Let Atul's sacrifice remind us that silence is complicity and that the fight for justice requires courage, resilience, and solidarity.

May Atul's soul rest in peace, and may his story inspire a future where justice is truly blind, and the law serves as a beacon of hope for all.

Save Indian Family Foundation

For Justice, For Equity, For All

https://www.saveindianfamily.org/

Acknowledgements

First of all, we are most thankful to the founders of Save Indian Family Foundation (SIFF), Anil Kumar Sir and Pandurang Katti Sir, as well as SIFF Coordinator Rajesh Vakharia Sir, for their amazing dedication and tireless hard work for many years in helping distressed men and raising awareness of men's rights.

We are thankful to Vijay Sahu, a SIFF volunteer and NIMHANS well-being volunteer, for useful suggestions related to this book.

Chapter 1: Atul's Story

1.1 The beginning of the nightmare

Atul's journey into a legal and emotional abyss began shortly after his marriage to Nikita, a highly educated woman working in a multinational company. What seemed like a promising union turned into a relentless series of disputes, accusations, and legal battles. Initially, the disagreements seemed minor—typical marital tiffs—but they soon escalated into something far more sinister.

The first blow came when Nikita left their Bengaluru home, taking their young son and filing multiple criminal cases against Atul and his family in Jaunpur. These included accusations of dowry harassment, unnatural sex, and even murder. Each case required Atul to travel to Uttar Pradesh repeatedly, disrupting his life and career in Bengaluru.

The demands began to mount. Nikita and her family sought extravagant sums in settlements, starting at ₹1 crore and later increasing to ₹3 crores. Atul found himself cornered by a system that seemed to favor his wife unconditionally, ignoring his evidence and pleas for justice. The strain on his finances and mental health began to show.

1.2 Trapped by the System

For Atul, the courtroom became a symbol of injustice. Judge Rita Kaushik, who presided over many of his cases, appeared indifferent to his plight. In his suicide note, he recounted incidents where the judge laughed at his desperation and openly demanded bribes. Atul described the court proceedings as a "bidding war," where those who paid the highest bribes secured favorable outcomes.

Despite submitting evidence of his innocence, Atul faced setbacks at every turn. His applications for video conferencing to avoid frequent travel were denied. Even after exposing contradictions in his wife's testimony, the judgments continued to favor her.

What made matters worse was the alienation from his son. Atul had not seen his child in three years, a fact that weighed heavily on him. He described the emotional toll of being labeled a villain in the eyes of the court, society, and even his own child.

1.3 The Legal Minefield

Atul's story is a stark illustration of how well-intentioned laws can be weaponized, turning the justice system into a theater of extortion and despair. Laws like Section 498A of the Indian Penal Code, originally designed to protect women from dowry harassment, have become tools for exploitation in the hands of some. Atul's life became a case study of this misuse.

The "False Cases Industry"

Atul's wife, Nikita, filed a series of cases, each more damaging than the last:

- **IPC 498A and Dowry Harassment**: Accusations included demands for dowry and physical abuse. However, Nikita later admitted under cross-examination that some allegations were filed without her knowledge.

- **Domestic Violence (DV)**: She sought ₹2 lakhs per month in maintenance, even though she was an independent professional earning a comfortable salary.

- **CrPC 125 (Maintenance)**: The court ordered ₹40,000 per month for their 2-year-old son, an amount Atul called "unrealistic and unjustified," especially in a city like Jaunpur.

Each of these cases required court appearances, consuming Atul's time, finances, and mental health. Over two years, he traveled to Jaunpur more than 40 times, often taking leave from work and incurring heavy expenses. His aging parents, too, were dragged into the legal quagmire, traveling from Bihar for court dates.

The Cost of Fighting Back

Atul's attempts to defend himself revealed systemic biases:

- **Corruption in the Judiciary**: Atul detailed how court staff demanded bribes even for scheduling routine hearings. The judge herself allegedly demanded ₹5 lakhs for a favorable settlement.

- **Legal Costs**: Lawyer fees, travel expenses, and missed work days mounted rapidly. Atul calculated that he had spent more fighting the cases than what was being demanded as maintenance.

- **Emotional Toll**: Beyond the financial strain, Atul struggled with the stigma of being accused. Friends and colleagues distanced themselves, leaving him increasingly isolated.

The judicial system, rather than offering respite, became a mechanism of harassment. Atul began to feel that justice was not just delayed but systematically denied.

1.4 Alienation and Despair

For Atul, the pain of being separated from his son eclipsed even the financial and legal challenges. In his suicide note, he described how his love for his child had been turned into a weapon against him.

A Father's Love, Exploited

Atul's son, Vyom, was only 1.5 years old when the cases began. Despite multiple applications for visitation rights, Atul was denied even basic contact with his child. His requests for video calls were ignored, and letters went unanswered.

Nikita's messages were explicit: "You will never see your son again." Atul realized that his son was being used as leverage in a cruel game of extortion. The court, far from facilitating reconciliation, seemed complicit in his alienation.

The Breaking Point

The alienation took a toll on Atul's identity as a father. He wrote in his note:

"When I first saw you, I thought I could give my life for you any day. But sadly, I am giving my life because of you."

Atul's anguish was compounded by his perception that the system valued his financial contributions over his emotional bond with his child. He felt reduced to a "wallet," a source of income to fund the very system that was oppressing him.

1.5 A System in Collapse

Atul's story reveals the cracks in India's judicial and social systems:

- **Misuse of Laws**: The unchecked filing of false cases has created a parallel "industry" where legal protections are weaponized for personal gain.

- **Judicial Corruption**: Bribes and favoritism erode trust in the courts, leaving genuine victims without recourse.

- **Neglect of Men's Rights**: Atul's case highlights the absence of safeguards for men falsely accused, particularly in family courts.

1.6 Corruption in the Halls of Justice

For Atul, the courtroom was not a place of solace but a battleground fraught with corruption and bias. His suicide note paints a damning picture of the judicial system in small-town India, particularly in Jaunpur Family Court, where he felt justice was systematically denied.

The Bribe Culture

Atul documented multiple instances where court officials openly demanded bribes:

- **Routine Bribes**: From ₹50 for scheduling a hearing to ₹5,000 for securing a more convenient court date, bribery was normalized in the system.

- **The Judge's Demand**: Atul alleged that Judge Rita Kaushik demanded ₹5 lakhs to settle the case. When he refused, she mocked his financial struggles and hinted at the long-drawn legal battles he would face without compliance.

Bias Against Men

Atul's plight was exacerbated by what he perceived as systemic gender bias:

- His wife's contradictory statements and false allegations were largely ignored or dismissed by the court.

- Even when evidence proved his innocence, judgments favored his wife, attributing higher maintenance demands based on his pre-tax income.

The Cost of Speaking Out

Atul's attempts to challenge corruption only deepened his despair. He detailed instances of unfair practices, from manipulated evidence to biased judgments. Each act of resistance was met with retaliation, reinforcing his belief that the system was irredeemably broken.

1.7 Weaponizing Parenthood

One of the most harrowing aspects of Atul's ordeal was the weaponization of his role as a father. His son, Vyom, became an unwitting pawn in a bitter legal and emotional battle.

The Price of Fatherhood

The court ordered Atul to pay ₹40,000 per month for his son's maintenance, an amount he called "unrealistic" given his financial responsibilities. Despite this, he was denied access to his child:

- Applications for visitation rights were delayed or ignored.

- His wife moved cities without informing him, further complicating his attempts to stay in contact.

The Emotional Fallout

Atul's suicide note captures his heartbreak:

"A father's love should never be reduced to a liability. But this system has turned my love for my son into a weapon of harassment."

He struggled with the emotional conflict of loving a child he could no longer see or protect. The alienation gnawed at his identity, leaving him feeling powerless and dehumanized.

1.8 The Family's Plight

Atul's death was not just his tragedy; it was a devastating blow to his family, who had already endured years of harassment and humiliation.

The Parents' Struggle

Atul's aging parents, residents of Bihar, were dragged into the legal quagmire:

- Multiple trips to Jaunpur for court dates, often to face baseless accusations.

- Emotional and financial strain as they supported Atul through his battles.

A Brother's Pain

Atul's brother, living in Delhi, was also implicated in the cases, despite having minimal interaction with Nikita. The baseless accusations created rifts within the family, adding to their collective suffering.

A Broken System

Atul's family became collateral damage in a system designed to protect. Their ordeal underscores the broader societal implications of legal misuse:

- Families of accused individuals often bear the brunt of harassment.

- The ripple effects of false cases extend beyond the immediate parties, fracturing relationships and eroding trust in the system.

1.9: The Social Cost of False Cases

Atul's story is not an isolated incident. It reflects a growing trend of misuse in family and dowry-related laws, which has profound societal implications.

The Rise of the "False Cases Industry"

Statistics show an alarming increase in cases filed under Section 498A, many of which are eventually proven false. This misuse undermines the credibility of genuine victims:

- False cases clog the judicial system, delaying justice for those who truly need it.

- The stigma surrounding false allegations affects not just the accused but also their families and communities.

The Need for Reform

Atul's case highlights the urgent need for judicial and legislative reforms:

- Stricter penalties for filing false cases to deter misuse.
- Gender-neutral laws to ensure fairness for all parties.
- Fast-track courts to reduce the backlog of family-related cases.

1.10 A Call to Action

Atul's death is a wake-up call for society, the judiciary, and policymakers. His story demands introspection and action to prevent similar tragedies.

Advocacy for Men's Rights

Atul's case has reignited debates about the rights of men in matrimonial disputes. Organizations advocating for men's rights emphasize:

- The psychological and emotional toll of false accusations.

- The need for equal treatment in family courts.

A Path Forward

Atul's note ends with a poignant plea for justice, not just for himself but for all those trapped in similar situations. His final wishes reflect a hope that his death will spark change:

- Greater transparency and accountability in the judiciary.

- A legal system that prioritizes truth and fairness over gender-based biases.

1.11 Conclusion: Atul's Legacy

Atul's story is a tragic reminder of the human cost of systemic failures. His struggle, documented in his suicide note, serves as a testament to the urgent need for reform. While his life ended in despair, his voice resonates as a powerful call for justice and change.

Chapter 2: Justice is Due: A Call for Judicial Reforms

JUSTICE IS DUE
A call for judicial reforms

Introduction

I woke up with a call on my mobile from my friend and as I picked it up, still in a sleepy mood, he said "Rajeeva, got to know? Atul committed suicide yesterday night". For a moment, I could not believe what I heard and as if to affirm my disbelief I asked "You mean to say he attempted?" "No. He's no more" came the answer.

By now this news is well, all over the social media, mainstream media, being discussed, debated. Some accounts belittled, even abused Atul for taking out his own life. There have been various demands from netizens ranging from calls to punish those who have been accused in his dying note - his wife and her relatives, the Principal Family Court Judge, Jaunpur who laughed at his situation when his wife asked him to commit suicide in open court. Some fringe radicals even were seen urging him to commit crime in harming the false accuser instead of committing suicide.

Time and again we come through cases where fathers commit suicide where they get separated from their children (Remember Syed Maqdoom's suicide video?[1]) let's admit it. The issue is not just about mothers not letting their children have some quality time with their fathers, but the active participation of the courts in institutionalized denial. Nor will #AtulSubhash be the last to face estrangement of his child as the situation is going to worsen before it starts to improve. Though the FIR has now been filed against all the names in Atul's suicide note, with the exception of the judge, we know well they will likely get bail, and in a few years mostly acquitted for "want of evidence" mostly as a repeat of Syed Maqdoom's case and others.

The deeper malaise

Atul's suicide note brings out a plethora of problems in our judicial system, which is not just limited to Atul's case. About 140000 cases of 498a are registered every year and are pretty high in some states like UP, Rajasthan & West Bengal.

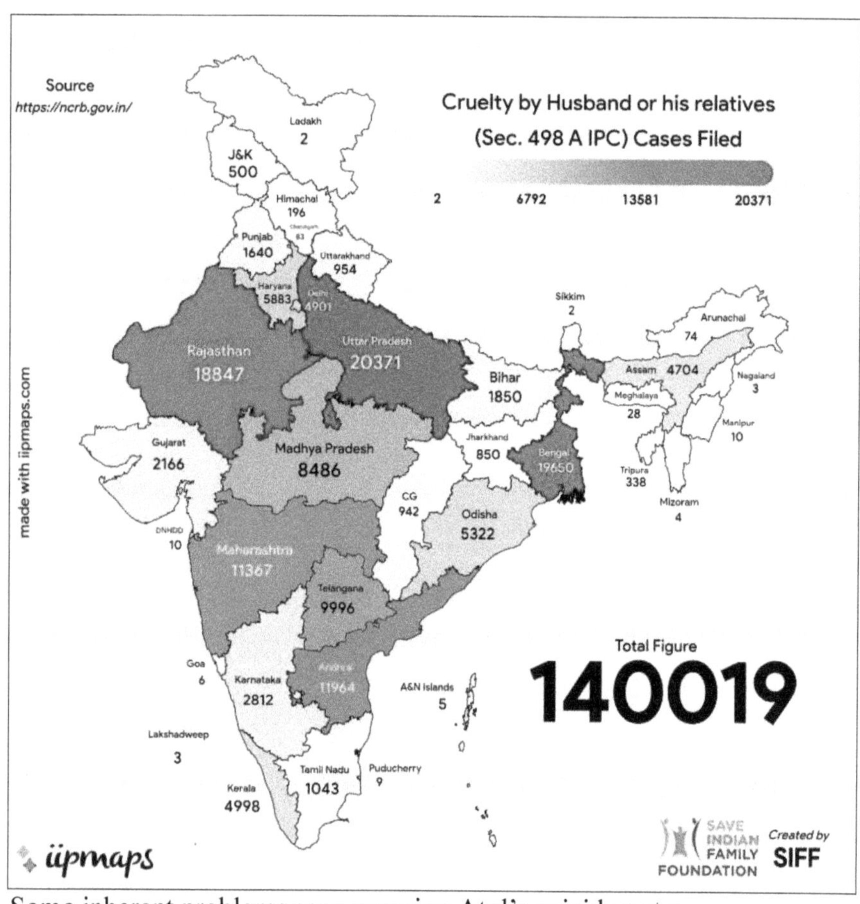

Some inherent problems seen perusing Atul's suicide note:

Issue of filing false cases

False cases ruining the lives of men and his family are not limited to marital discords. People who do not enter the wedlock and prefer a live-in relationship thinking at least their families cannot be implicated in a 498a case - they get rape cases filed against them instead. India should probably the only country in the world where refusal to marry after having consensual sex is considered rape. Earlier it was filed under IPC375 (Rape). BNS has a separate section 69 explicitly criminalizing non-marriage even after "consensual" sex. Forced marriages due to threat of rape is quietly, but quickly becoming the new norm. What does society expect in such marriages, where the man was forced to marry despite the relationship having broken down? Does society or the legal system think that once they marry they will have a "Happy married life" ?

Then there is issue of POSH (Prevention of sexual harassment at workplace). It's not long ago that VP of Genpact Swaroop committed suicide[2]. One unsubstantiated allegation at office is sufficient to destroy the entire career of a man (and his life too in some cases).

Even young boys are not spared from this menace. A 14 year old boy Manav, jumped from 11th floor after allegations of sexual harassment on instagram.[3] Many times, we see minor or just major boys and girls who explore sex without being aware of its ramifications. In such cases the boy is arrested under POCSO even if the girl is older[4]. With the amendment of the juvenile justice act, the minor boy is tried as an adult and might get lodged in adult prisons too! What are the chances this minor boy might come out of an adult prison after serving his sentence as a hardcore criminal, considering his contacts in adult prisons.

The issue of filing false cases is not even limited to personal relationships or people you might have an acquaintance with. A completely random woman can accuse a man of sexual misconduct and act with impunity as witnessed in Sarvajit's case[5] or a molestation case as in Rohtak Sisters case[6]. In the latter case, the young men who intended to join the army were debarred from sitting for the written exam and when they finally got acquitted, they had crossed the age bar !

The process itself is the harassment

In particular, litigations related to marital cases can have what I wish to term "multi-tiered litigation". Multiple cases can be filed and they are tried in different courts. E.g criminal cases in JMFC courts, civil disputes related to divorce/custody in family courts and in many cities domestic violence under traffic courts (Did I say traffic courts for domestic violence cases? Its true !!!). Add the complications if these cases are in various cities. One at the place where either the man or the woman belong to, one where they got married and one at the place they lived after marriage. All these cases can have different dates. In criminal cases, one date of non-appearance of a man can lead to issuance of NBW (Non-bailable warrant) while the woman (the accuser) need not attend the court dates for years. Keeping in mind that the man has to mandatorily attend the criminal cases, he needs to apply for leave at the workplace for every date. (40 dates in Atul's case while he was entitled to 23 leaves in his company !). Not to forget additional time he needs to travel to a different state. Ok. One reaches the court. What happens on that date? You get a new date and this whole cycle has to be repeated every time !! Adjournments have become the norm in our courts, popularly called as #TareeqPeTareeq in the legal fraternity.

What about visitation?

United Nations Convention on the Rights of the Child, which India has ratified on 11.12.1992, i.e., Article 7 of UNCRC: "the right to know and be cared for by their parents".According to article 8,9,10 of the UNCRC 1989 every child has the right to maintain uninterrupted direct and personal relation & contact with both the parents even if the parents are separated. I do not understand how our country/judicial system could act so irresponsibly on this matter considering India having ratified the right of a child to maintain contact with its separated parent. Very many cases galore where parents separated when the child was still an infant, by the time a father secures access to "Visit" his own child, the innocent child does not even recognize its father. Some children have addressed their fathers as "Uncle". Much worse, some mothers take undue advantage to vilify their father and as a consequence say "I hate you" when they see their father for the first time in years. We in SIFF come across many such fathers who have bitterly cried the night or lost sleep when these kinds of incidents happened in their lives. There is little psychologists can do in such cases. #AtulSubhash just happened to be one of them.

The issue of "settlement"

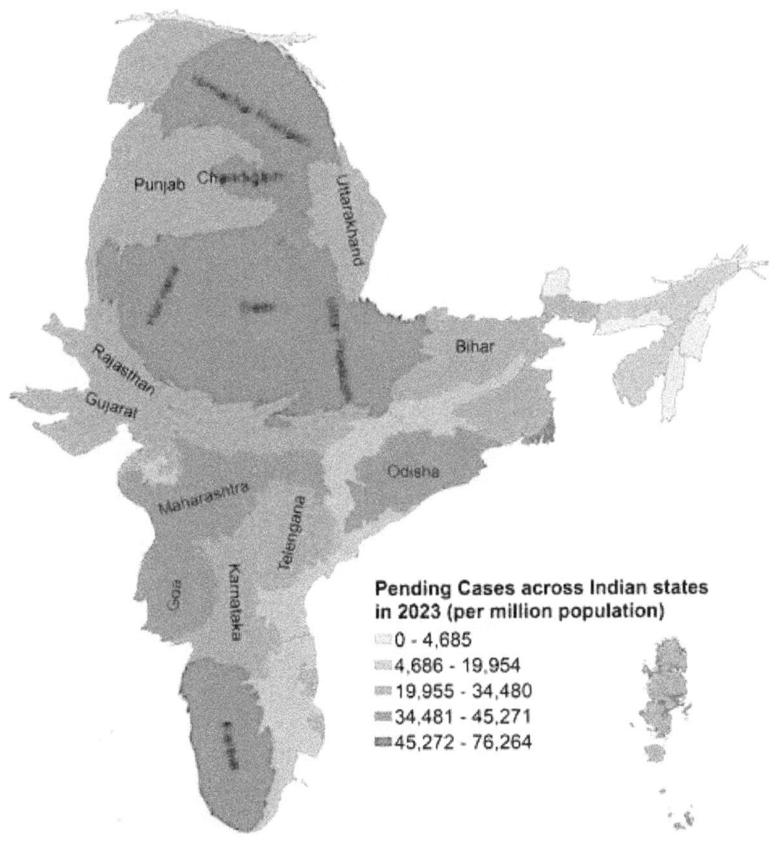

District courts: 43 million out of a total of 49 million cases

Subordinate courts: 44 million cases, a 38% increase from 2019

High courts: 6.1 million cases in 2023

Supreme Court: 83,000 cases pending

[7]

Considering the enormous number of cases that are in pending state, the courts came up with mediation centres or officially alternative dispute resolution (ADR) sometime in 2005. Now depending on the mutual agreement of the parties, they could "settle" the matter in court-annexed mediation Centre. The website of mediation centres list down the supposedly "benefits" to the litigants and the lawyers, reduce the burden of cases for courts.

While this mechanism has come in handy for litigants to get out of their cases, this mechanism can be effectively used by unscrupulous litigants to wreak havoc on the other party. Now an alimony that might get awarded though due process in courts, which might take years can be negotiated at will, while there is no upper limit on what a litigant "wants" to close the cases, nor does judiciary take any accountability for the extravagant demands asked by a litigant in the mediation process. The mediation centres have turned into institutionalized extortion centres and it's not limited to marital disputes alone. Landlord-tenant, illegal occupation of empty land, descendants filing a claim on land after the sale of ancestral land, cheque bounces all cases now in one way or the other end up in mediation centres and the matter is "settled".

This is now a huge problem. Not only can we NOT filter out genuine cases from the false cases, the statistics collected at NCRB includes mediation assisted settled cases as "acquitted". This system now can not only be misused, but can be rampantly abused too. The modus-operandi is always to file a false case, extort money as settlement in the mediation center attached to the court and repeat the same cycle in other courts and cities. The accused, fearing their reputation tarnished or to avoid a complicated legal battle simply give in to extortion. Since the judicial system is lethargic and completely devoid of technological infrastructure, it can take ages to detect such a pattern and only comes out rare in catching such culprits.[8]

Woman arrested in Jaipur for filing multiple rape complaints for 'extrotion'

According to the police, the woman filed over a dozen rape cases against a lawyer to extort money from him by blackmailing him. In the past, she has also filed at least 15 FIRs against different people in several parts of the country.

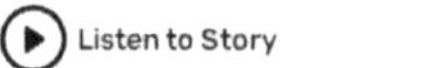

In the particular case of marital discord, a wife can literally file a plethora of cases against the husband and his family, in the cities she wishes to and use the mediation centres to extort at will, while she has literally nothing to lose - while not forgetting the use of children as tools for blackmail. In other cases, wait for the court to grant an interim maintenance and depending on the quantum ordered, raise the amount for alimony/settlement. In the zealous race to push litigants to go for a mediation and settle up the matter and get the pending cases out of their bucket, judges coerce, issue a veiled threat, or sometimes openly threaten dire consequences. And this is exactly what we see in Atul's case. Pasting some snippets from his suicide note (Highlight is my emphasis):

Judge: Ye case settle kyu nahi kar lete
Me: Ma'am, Ye log pehle 1 Crore ki demand kar rahe the, aapke interim maintenance ke order ke baad 3 Crore ki demand kar rahe hai
Judge: Phir honge tumhare pas 3 crore. Isliye maang rahi hai

Judge: Ye cases sab jhuthey hote hai. Aisa hi hota hai. Tum apne aur apni family ke baare me socho. Ye cases settle kar lo. Hum tumhari help karenge.
Me: Theek hai Ma'am, aap suggest karo. Lekin mere pas itne paise nahi hai
Judge: Hum adjust karayenge, mai **Rs 5 lakh** lungi, aur mai settle kara dungi. Issi court me sab settle ho jayega. Bahut hi reasonable amount hai, itna paisa kamate ho tum. Nikita bhi adjust karegi. Nahi to jeewan bhar tum aur tumhare maa baap court kachehri ke chakkar kaat te rahenge.

Does the judiciary really not care?

At this point in time, it can be safely said that the judiciary , especially high courts and supreme courts, are simply not in a mood to give any relief to men. The parties who approached them to get some kind of relief or protection from such harassment in courts have either been punished with a fine or simply dismissed. No wonder public trended #JudiciaryHatesMen after Atul's news came out.

A bitter PIL in HC: Suing against 'cruel women',man fined Rs 1 lakh

The Gujarat High Court on Thursday slapped a fine of Rs 1 lakh to one Dashrath Devda who had filed a petition demanding legal protection to men against alleged harassment by women.

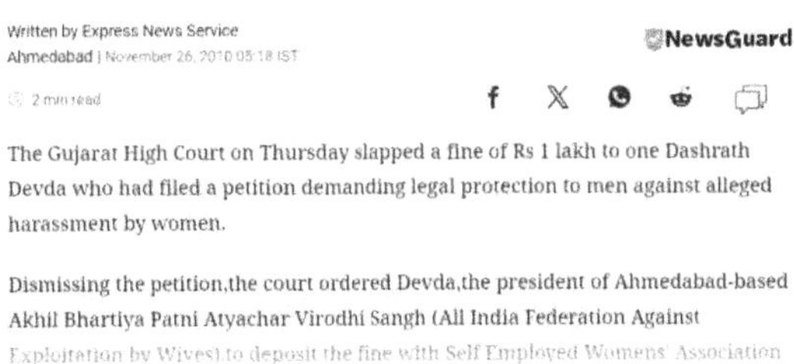

Written by Express News Service
Ahmedabad | November 26, 2010 05:18 IST

2 min read

The Gujarat High Court on Thursday slapped a fine of Rs 1 lakh to one Dashrath Devda who had filed a petition demanding legal protection to men against alleged harassment by women.

Dismissing the petition,the court ordered Devda,the president of Ahmedabad-based Akhil Bhartiya Patni Atyachar Virodhi Sangh (All India Federation Against Exploitation by Wives) to deposit the fine with Self Employed Womens' Association

Do You Want An Association For People Who May Commit Suicide In Future: SC Asks While Dismissing PIL Seeking Commission For Men

By - Ramey Krishan Rana

Update: 2023-07-03 08:00 GMT

The present situation reminds me of senior advocate Dushyant Dave arguing in favor of the National Judicial Appointments Commission (NJAC) lamented and below are his words.

"My Lords should wear a burqa and roam in the court corridors to hear the way lawyers talk about the judges of this court. You will get first-hand account of the rotting justice delivery system. The kind of lawyers who are being appointed as judges is a disgrace,"

That said, it is also the SC that stepped in, lamenting of misuse of provisions, the latest ironically yesterday[9]. However, in spite of these landmark judgments, the ground realities have not changed a bit for the better. While the courts often give sweeping directions – ones that get bold headlines, ones that raise hope among citizens – they do not as often follow these up to see whether the Executive has carried them out. If the officials concerned had not suffered in the least for not obeying the landmark judgment the Supreme Court itself delivered 20 years earlier, why would they follow the directives now? These directives have thus far remained on paper.

The way forward; What should common citizens do?

Of the four pillars in our democracy, there is some kind of accountability and cleanup in three of them. Journalists get demoted, politicians are elected out and bureaucracy face suspensions, raids, transfers to posts of lesser importance etc. However, the fourth pillar, the judiciary, has the least accountability. One reason is the tougher process to file complaints against judges which require the explicit permission of CJ's. It's compounded by the fact that the collegium system has appointed one of "their own" and complaints even if taken up could land up to a judge who is an acquaintance of the complained. While the present govt proposed NJAC bill, the govt chickened out after SC declared it unconstitutional. The citizens should pressurize the parliament to bring in some kind of judicial accountability and should be put in action.

Use technology as a measure to bring relief

#DigitalIndia is a well marketed campaign, while the courts today are in a state which cannot work without paper. Govt should infuse funds to make judiciary tech savvy. There should be no need for litigants to come every date physically to the courts. Courts should allow video conferencing as the default option and in exceptional cases like say cross, or to take an oath make physical appearance mandatory. That way, courts will be less crowded. The proceedings and filing applications, interim and responses, defense could be just uploaded to a digital platform. The history of the litigations a person was involved in should be captured in a database and strictly used to determine the conduct of a litigant.

It has to be noted that having cutting edge tech alone is not going to solve the problem without fixing process issues. What is the point of investing in tech if courts still give #TareeqPeTareeq? Adjournments should be limited to say three per litigant per case. Have a single-window court system for all cases between two litigants. Shared parenting should be the default norm and should be the first to get executed on ground, ensuring the relationship of the child is not broken with the non-custodial parent.

Most importantly, separate the seeds from chaff in the case filing stage. The courts need to put an end to taking up cases bereft of any evidence. If courts are getting burdened with pending cases, it is mostly due to the fearlessness of those who misuse and abuse the system, knowing fully well that courts do take up perjury cases rarely and the ease in which women can file such cases on vague allegations. If the courts are serious enough to tackle this issue, they should crack down on those who wantonly misused the provisions, lied to the court on oath of perjury. Action should be taken against lawyers who regularly use such tactics by, say , cancelling their bar license?

Finally on the issue of mediation centres and the issue of settlement. Mediation centres should discourage exorbitant demands and factor in elements like duration of the marriage, wife's contribution to the marriage etc to see if the "settlement" demand is reasonable. In short, people approach courts to get justice. Today, the irony is that most cases ending up in settlement through mediation centres is seen as a "successful" model and not as inefficiency of the judicial system.

It is hoped that sacrifice of #AtulSubhash does not go waste and we as a society start to reform our institutions in a civilized manner.

The author is a techie by profession and tweets @rajeevmysore

References

[1] https://bangaloremirror.indiatimes.com/bangalore/others/separated-from-son-techie-hangs-himself/articleshow/22174260.cms

[2] https://www.indiatoday.in/india/story/top-genpact-executive-commits-suicide-in-noida-over-accusations-of-sexual-harassment-1413409-2018-12-20

[3] https://www.freepressjournal.in/india/my-brother-is-not-a-rapist-sibling-of-gurugram-teen-who-committed-suicide-writes-emotional-note-says-not-related-to-bois-locker-room

[4] https://zeenews.india.com/india/12-year-old-boy-booked-under-pocso-act-for-raping-impregnating-17-year-old-girl-in-tamil-nadu-2456161.html

[5] https://www.indiatoday.in/india/story/complaint-doubtful-delhi-court-acquits-sarvjeet-singh-in-2015-sexual-harassment-case-1613088-2019-10-26

[6] http://www.ndtv.com/india-news/court-ends-case-against-3-rohtak-molesters-girls-may-appeal-order-1666224

[7] Image and data credits: https://doi.org/10.1080/21681376.2024.2425328

[8] https://www.indiatoday.in/cities/jaipur/story/woman-arrested-in-jaipur-for-filing-false-rape-complaint-for-extrotion-2541220-2024-05-20

[9] https://www.barandbench.com/news/section-498a-being-misused-force-husband-comply-wifes-unreasonable-demands-supreme-court

Chapter 3: How to Save the Next Atul

I did not have much chance to interact with Atul, but I did meet him last year a few times and chatted with him over lunch. He seemed a pretty intelligent, determined, and well-adjusted person with lots of friends, a nice job in a good company, and earning good money. He was just 34. His death was indeed shocking to me and to all of us.

On hearing about his death, the first thought that came to me was sadness at the loss of such a bright young man, full of promise. It is such an unnecessary loss of a productive and intelligent person, a huge loss to the whole country. India definitely needs his type of people to build the nation and contribute their time and efforts to growing the economy till we become a developed nation.

As per NCRB data, thousands of young men commit suicide every year due to matrimonial disputes - often triggered by false cases and the misuse of laws. It is a pitiful waste of the nation's precious human resources. Thankfully, Atul's sacrifice seems to have spurred a lot of people to feel outrage and even forced the major TV and news channels to cover it, which is rare for suicides by young men. Therefore, his sacrifice was absolutely not in vain.

However, I firmly believe we must do everything possible to prevent such extreme actions. For every Atul whose tragic story reaches the headlines, there are countless others suffering in silence, harassed by India's slow-moving, corruption-infested, and inefficient justice system. One of the teachers at the NIMHANS Center for Well Being, whom I respect greatly, once said, *"Every suicide is really a call for help."* This means that every person contemplating suicide can be saved if they receive the right support at the right time.

Recognizing the Signs of Someone in Danger

It is often said that those who are most in need of help rarely ask for it outright. This is especially true for men in India, who are conditioned to suppress their emotions and endure hardships silently. Here are a few signs to watch for:

- **Withdrawal from Social Circles**: Someone who was once active and sociable may suddenly start avoiding friends, family, and social gatherings.

- **Increased Irritability or Despair**: Frequent expressions of hopelessness, frustration, or despair, especially about legal, financial, or personal issues.

- **Talking About Death or Escape**: Remarks such as "I can't take this anymore," or "It would be better if I just disappeared," can indicate deeper struggles.

- **Changes in Behavior**: Drastic changes in routines, such as neglecting work, hygiene, or hobbies they once enjoyed.

- **Overwhelming Financial Strain**: Constant worries about legal expenses, maintenance payments, or other financial pressures.

How to Help Someone Like Atul

If you recognize someone showing these signs, here are a few ways you can help:

- **Offer a Listening Ear:** Sometimes, all a person needs is someone who listens without judgment. Let them vent their frustrations, fears, and feelings without interruption or advice. Simply being there can make a significant difference.

- **Encourage Professional Help:** Recommend counseling or therapy. Organizations like NIMHANS and suicide prevention helplines offer affordable and confidential support. Normalize seeking help and accompany them if needed.

- **Help Them Navigate Resources:** Men in matrimonial disputes often feel isolated. Direct them to NGOs like **Save Indian Family Foundation (SIFF)**, which provide legal advice, emotional support, and a sense of community to men facing false cases.

- **Reduce Their Isolation**: Encourage them to reengage with social activities or hobbies. Offer to spend time with them - whether it is a casual walk, a movie night, or even helping them with errands.

- **Take Suicidal Comments Seriously**: If someone talks about ending their life, never dismiss it as a joke or exaggeration. Encourage them to share their thoughts, and if necessary, seek immediate professional intervention.

- **Advocate for Systemic Change:** Join campaigns to raise awareness about the misuse of laws like Section 498A, the rights of fathers and men generally and advocate for judicial reforms. Support organizations that fight for fairness in matrimonial cases to ensure fewer people face Atul's plight in the future.

Building a Support System for Men

We also need to create a culture where men can express vulnerability without fear of judgment. Society must recognize that mental health struggles and harassment affect men as much as women, and support systems must be accessible to all, irrespective of gender.

Atul's sacrifice was a wake-up call, but let us not wait for another tragedy to act. We must save the next Atul by being vigilant, offering support, and pushing for systemic change. Together, we can ensure that no bright life is lost to despair, and no family has to mourn the loss of a son, brother, or father to a broken system.

Let's remember Atul by making this world a fairer, kinder, and more just place.

The author is a techie, researcher and well-being volunteer and tweets @joyboseroy

Chapter 4: Marital Cases and Timely Resolution

This chapter highlights the critical need for marital disputes to be resolved within a fixed time frame. Prolonged cases often hinder personal growth, trapping individuals in emotional and legal limbo. The chapter explores how timely resolutions can provide a fresh start, enabling affected parties to rebuild their lives and focus on their well-being. It underscores the importance of streamlined legal processes, mediation, and judicial efficiency to prevent emotional fatigue and ensure justice is served promptly, fostering a healthier society.

If marital cases are not resolved within a fixed timeframe, it can have devastating psychological consequences, including fostering suicidal thoughts in a person's mind. The prolonged uncertainty and emotional strain of unresolved disputes often lead to feelings of hopelessness, isolation, and despair. As individuals remain trapped in legal and emotional limbo, their ability to focus on personal growth or rebuild their lives diminishes, further compounding their mental anguish. Timely resolution of such cases is not just a matter of legal efficiency but a crucial step toward safeguarding mental health and ensuring individuals can move forward with dignity and purpose.

Never blame the person who has taken their own life due to the overwhelming burden of prolonged marital cases. Such tragedies are a reflection of a system that fails to provide timely resolution and compassionate support. Instead of assigning blame to the victim, society must focus on reforming the system to make it more empathetic and efficient. This includes implementing fixed timeframes for case resolution, offering accessible mental health support, and fostering a process that prioritizes the well-being of individuals. By addressing the root causes of such despair, we can create a system that uplifts and protects those navigating challenging marital disputes.

Men often bear a significant financial burden in various aspects of life, including heavy income taxes, monthly maintenance payments granted to their wives in marital disputes, and indirect taxes on goods and services. This financial strain is further compounded by the rising costs of daily necessities, such as increased bus fares and other transportation expenses. These cumulative obligations can create immense pressure, leaving little room for personal savings or investments. Addressing these challenges requires a fair and balanced system that ensures financial responsibilities are equitably distributed, alleviating undue stress and fostering economic stability for all individuals.

Karma and Bhagya issue - Instead upgrade your system

Don't blame karma and bhagya (destiny) for the shortcomings of a failed system. While these beliefs may offer solace, they should not be used to excuse systemic inefficiencies that impact countless lives. A failing judicial system, marked by delays and inequities, calls for urgent reform rather than resignation to fate. By upgrading the judicial process to be more efficient, transparent, and people-centric, we can create a framework that ensures justice is served promptly and fairly. A society that invests in better governance and accountability paves the way for collective progress and the well-being of its citizens.

Save time for young innovators

When young people are forced to spend their valuable time entangled in prolonged marital disputes, it results in a significant loss not only to their personal growth but also to the nation. This loss of productivity and potential innovation weakens the social and economic fabric, as the energy and creativity of youth are diverted toward navigating a failed judicial system rather than contributing to progress. Time is a precious resource that should be channeled into innovation, education, and nation-building. Reforming the judicial system to provide swift resolutions is essential for empowering individuals and fostering a society that thrives on productivity and advancement.

Need for a logical judicial system

Introducing logical subjects and rigorous mathematics into LLB passing exams can significantly enhance the analytical and decision-making skills of aspiring lawyers and judges. These disciplines train the mind to approach problems systematically, evaluate evidence critically, and construct sound arguments. A strong foundation in logic and mathematics ensures that legal professionals are not only well-versed in laws but also equipped with the intellectual tools to interpret them fairly and effectively. By integrating such subjects into the curriculum, we can nurture a generation of legal experts capable of delivering justice with precision, clarity, and rationality, thereby strengthening the judicial system.

Need for a life of dignity for loyal taxpayers - Atul's worry

Atul, an AI engineer, tragically took his own life amidst the overwhelming pressures of a marital case. The relentless cycle of court visits, coupled with the demands of a fast-paced and challenging job, left him frustrated and exhausted. Living in a metro city, Atul had to physically travel long distances to attend court hearings in a distant village, further straining his ability to balance work and personal commitments. In his suicide video, he expressed deep frustration, particularly about the tax system, which he felt was working against him despite his contributions. Sadly, Atul's story is not unique; it echoes the struggles of many young men entangled in marital disputes that drag on for years, leaving them emotionally and financially drained.

Chapter 5: A Tragic Wake Up Call: The Life and Death of Atul Subhash

It was an ordinary morning when my world tilted off its axis. Around 10:00 AM, while chatting with Joy Bose, I received devastating news: Atul Subhas, a dedicated member of the *Save Indian Family Foundation* (SIFF), had taken his own life in his Bangalore apartment. A late-night WhatsApp message from Atul, stating his intent to end his life, had circulated among SIFF groups. He implored anyone nearby to visit his home, but by the time help arrived, it was too late.

I frantically reached out to a long-time SIFF member who was at the scene. His voice was heavy with grief and disbelief as he described the grim reality: the police were collecting evidence while delicately handling the matter with Atul's parents, who were told he had been hospitalized. This small act of kindness did little to blunt the shock of the tragedy.

A Note That Shook the Soul

Later that day, as I attempted to focus on work, my phone buzzed with a PDF of Atul's suicide note. At 24 pages, it was meticulously detailed—a heartbreaking chronicle of his pain, laid out with dates and events in painstaking order. Every word carried the weight of his anguish, and every sentence revealed the systemic indifference he faced.

The note contained chilling quotes from those who contributed to his despair:

Judge: *"To kya ho gaya, cases daal diye to. Tumhari patni hai."* (*So what if cases have been filed? She's your wife.*)

Wife: *"To tum bhi suicide kyu nahi kar lete?"* (*Why don't you just kill yourself too?*)

Mother-in-law: *"Arey, tum abhi tak suicide nahi kiye? Mujhe laga aaj tumhare suicide ki khabar aayegi."* (*Oh, you still haven't killed yourself? I thought we'd hear about your suicide today.*)

These words weren't just cruel; they embodied the arrogance of those exploiting a system rigged against men. Atul's story mirrored countless discussions from SIFF meetings—stories of police apathy, judicial delays, and systemic bias that leave men in hopeless situations.

A Father's Heartache

The most harrowing part of Atul's note was his message to his son, Vyom. It encapsulated the unspeakable agony of a father alienated from his child:

"I can sacrifice 100 sons like you for my father. I can sacrifice 1,000 of myself for you."

This was not just a father's lament but a desperate cry against a system that reduces fathers to mere bystanders in their children's lives. Atul's son, like many children caught in the crossfire of parental disputes, had become a pawn in an emotionally and financially draining game. Mothers often weaponize children to demand alimony or child support, further isolating fathers. Courts, rather than mediating fairly, frequently exacerbate this alienation.

Atul's plea wasn't just for his son—it was for all children to see the love their fathers hold for them, despite being painted as villains by an unjust system.

A Fight Against Indifference

After digesting the contents of the note, I shared it with others and followed its spread across social media. Initially, hope seemed futile. Men's suicides are often dismissed as mere outcomes of depression, with no acknowledgment of the systemic issues driving them. Statements by prominent figures like Maneka Gandhi (*"Never heard or read of men committing suicide"*) and Renuka Chowdhury (*"It's time for men to suffer"*) highlight the deep-seated apathy towards male victims of injustice.

However, technology became a beacon of hope. Social media platforms like Twitter amplified Atul's story, sparking discussions about biased laws and judicial inefficiencies. Despite initial reluctance from mainstream media, the incident gained momentum as it trended online.

By evening, national TV channels and newspapers began covering the tragedy, forcing a nationwide conversation about the systemic bias men face.

The Systemic Failure

Atul's death is not an isolated incident. It is symptomatic of a society that fails to address the plight of men ensnared by outdated and prejudiced laws. Domestic violence, dowry harassment, and custody battles are arenas where men are often presumed guilty until proven innocent. Judges grant adjournments instead of justice, while some lawyers exploit the situation for financial gain. Meanwhile, fathers are alienated from their children, and men are vilified in the public eye.

This systemic apathy is compounded by the silence of feminist organizations, many of which fail to acknowledge injustices against men. While men have always stood in solidarity with women's causes—be it during the Nirbhaya case or other gender-based movements—when it comes to men's rights, these organizations often retreat into silence.

The Call to Act

Atul's death is a wake-up call. His 45-page note is not just a personal outcry; it is a manifesto for change. It demands that we, as a society, confront the biases in our legal and social systems. The movement for men's rights is not about opposing women's rights; it is about ensuring fairness for all.

Today, it was Atul. Tomorrow, it could be someone you know—a son, a brother, or a father. Let us not wait for the fire to reach our own homes. Let us honor Atul's sacrifice by fighting for a system that listens to everyone, irrespective of gender.

Atul Subhash did not end his life in vain. He made the ultimate sacrifice to shine a light on the darkness many endure. Let his story be the beginning of a broader conversation and a catalyst for change.

The author is a techie, a financial expert as well as a NIMHANS well-being volunteer. His handle is @VJYounMe

Chapter 6: The Aftermath of Tragedy: Unveiling Systemic Flaws in Matrimonial Justice

The next day, under mounting public and media pressure, the police filed an abetment to suicide case against Atul Subhas's wife and her family. Strikingly, the FIR excluded Judge Rita Kaushik, despite Atul explicitly naming her in his note as a key figure in his suffering. The omission raised serious questions about accountability within the judicial system.

A Hollow Framework for Alimony

Amid public outrage, the Supreme Court introduced an eight-point framework to guide courts in deciding alimony in divorce cases. While intended to appear as progress, the framework recycled familiar points without addressing fundamental flaws in the system. The guidelines emphasized:

- Social and financial status of both parties.
- Reasonable needs of the wife and dependent children.
- Qualifications and employment status of both spouses.
- Independent income or assets owned by the applicant.
- Standard of living during the marriage.
- Career sacrifices made by either spouse for family responsibilities.
- Litigation expenses for a non-working wife.
- The husband's financial capacity, including liabilities.

Critics quickly pointed out that the framework ignored critical issues. For instance, the duration of the marriage remained irrelevant, leaving men vulnerable regardless of whether a union lasted two days or two decades. Furthermore, the framework failed to define a wife's responsibilities or accountability, perpetuating a one-sided expectation of men as financial providers.

Deepening Injustice: Key Questions

The systemic bias in matrimonial laws raises pressing concerns:

- **Lack of Accountability for Wives**: Why are husbands solely responsible for maintaining wives, even those who label them as abusers? Courts often reward baseless accusations, encouraging misuse of the system.

- **Burden of Litigation Costs**: Why should husbands bear the legal expenses of their wives, especially when feminist organizations receive substantial funding to support women's causes? Could the government not provide legal aid to truly destitute women instead?

- **Unconditional Maintenance**: Why should wives enjoy the lifestyle of a matrimonial home without fulfilling their duties? Shouldn't maintenance decisions await the resolution of cases rather than punishing men preemptively?

- **Discouraging Male Productivity**: Linking maintenance to a husband's income discourages career growth. Why is a man's hard-earned money handed to someone who contributes neither to the family nor the economy?

- **Parental Alienation and Financial Exploitation**: Denying fathers access to their children while demanding child support is fundamentally unjust. Fathers should be granted unconditional access to their children if they are required to provide financial support.

A Nation in Mourning

The third day after Atul's death saw a wave of protests and condolence gatherings across major cities, including Bangalore, Delhi, Hyderabad, and Kolkata. In Delhi, peaceful mourners were met with arrests—a deeply disheartening response to a moment of collective grief. While some national media outlets covered the protests, the coverage lacked depth and urgency, revealing a broader unwillingness to confront systemic issues.

Feminist organizations, notably absent, neither supported Atul's family nor engaged in the public debate. This silence contrasted sharply with men's visible solidarity during women's rights movements, such as the Nirbhaya case.

Adding to the outrage, IT giant Accenture locked its official social media accounts as public pressure mounted to dismiss Atul's wife. Even the company's CEO, Julie Sweet, locked her profile amidst growing criticism.

Tragic Repercussions and A Broken System

Atul's death triggered a chain reaction. The following day brought more reports of suicides:

1. **Arvind Bharti** in Delhi, who filed a police complaint accusing his wife of false allegations before ending his life.

2. **Dr. Ajay Kumar** in Rajasthan, whose note blamed his wife for his despair.

3. **Navratan Singh, Pradeep Singh, and their mother**, a family from Rajasthan, who died by suicide amidst allegations of systemic failure to address their plight.

These incidents highlight a troubling reality: the system not only fails to deliver justice but also perpetuates cycles of despair and tragedy.

The Irony of "Justice"

In a glaring contradiction, on the same day the Supreme Court introduced its eight-point framework, it ordered a staggering Rs. 5 crore one-time alimony to a wife and Rs. 1 crore to an adult son in a 20-year-old divorce case. The case involved a young banker who married in 1998, separated in 2004, and spent two decades embroiled in family courts, high courts, and the Supreme Court. This decision, widely criticized, underscored the ineffectiveness of the new guidelines in addressing systemic inequities.

A Way Forward

The injustices in matrimonial laws demand urgent reform. Potential solutions include:

- **Pre-Marital Agreements**: Borrowing from Muslim marriage laws, couples could agree on maintenance terms before marriage, ensuring clarity and fairness.

- **Accountability for False Allegations**: Punish wives, lawyers, and families who file false cases, discouraging misuse of legal provisions.

- **Government and NGO Support**: Shift financial responsibility for destitute wives to government programs or NGOs, rather than burdening men.

- **Eliminate Pre-Trial Maintenance**: Remove monetary rewards during unresolved disputes, drastically reducing the incentive for frivolous cases.

- **Child Custody Reforms**: Grant fathers equal access to their children, aligning financial responsibilities with parental rights.

A Call to Action

Atul's death is more than an individual tragedy—it is a wake-up call for systemic reform. His sacrifice should inspire a movement to demand balanced laws that protect all parties in matrimonial disputes. Men, too, deserve fairness, dignity, and justice.

Let us honor Atul's memory by addressing the inequities in our legal system. Let his story, and the stories of those like him, spark a transformation toward a more just and compassionate society.

The author is a techie, a financial expert as well as a NIMHANS well-being volunteer. His handle is @VJYounMe

Chapter 7: Media Coverage of Atul's Death

In this chapter, we discuss a few articles related to Atul's suicide that have appeared in various media sources.

Zee News

https://zeenews.india.com/india/can-sacrifice-a-1000-of-me-for-you-techie-atul-subhashs-heart-wrenching-letter-to-his-minor-son-before-dying-word-by-word-2830078.html

Mint

https://www.livemint.com/news/trends/techie-in-bengaluru-dies-by-suicide-leaves-24-page-note-blaming-wife-her-family-justice-is-due-11733817488438.html

Techie in Bengaluru dies by suicide, leaves 24-page note blaming wife & her family: 'Justice is due'

Atul Subhash, 34, died by suicide in Bengaluru after legal troubles with his wife. A 24-page death note accused her and her family of harassment.

Written By **Arshdeep Kaur**

Updated • 10 Dec 2024, 02:08 PM IST

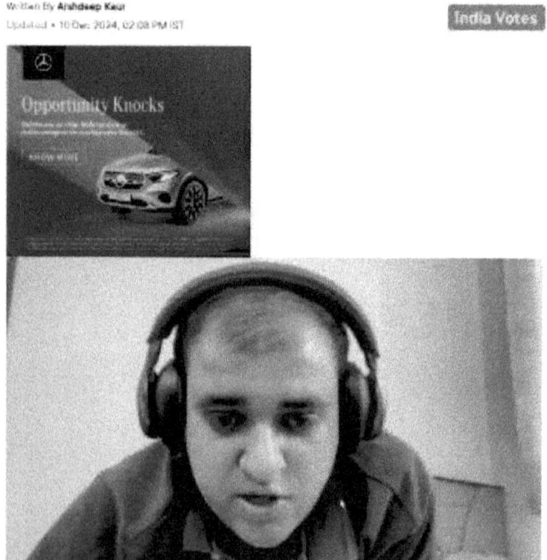

According to Atul Subhash's note, his wife was already receiving ₹40,000 every month as maintenance, despite working and earning her own money.

Atul Subhash, a 34-year-old techie, was found hanging in his Bengaluru home on Monday. According to police, Atul died by suicide and left a 24-page death note.

Originally from Uttar Pradesh, the techie lived in Manjunath Layout in Marathahalli police station limits in Bengaluru. He worked as a senior executive for a private firm in the city and had been living alone after separating from his wife.

The suicide note found at Atul's house had four handwritten pages, while the other 20 pages were typed out.

Economic Times

https://economictimes.indiatimes.com/news/india/bengaluru-executive-commits-suicide-after-sending-24-page-email-to-ngo-blaming-unending-harassment-by-wife/articleshow/116168475.cms?from=mdr

Bengaluru executive dies by suicide after sending 24-page email to NGO, blaming unending harassment by wife

ET Online · Last Updated: Dec 10, 2024, 07:39:00 PM IST

Synopsis

A 34-year-old executive, Atul Subhash, was found dead in his Bengaluru apartment after allegedly facing domestic violence charges. Atul left a 24-page suicide note and emailed an NGO detailing his ordeal before taking his life. Police discovered a message on his body and instructions for after his death. The news about the tragic incident has gone viral.

Bengaluru techie ends life, blames wife, judge; netizens ask, 'When will system wake up?'

In a tragic incident, Atul Subhash, a 34-year-old director-level executive from Uttar Pradesh, was found hanging in his apartment in Munnekolalu, Marathahalli, on Monday morning. Atul, who had been fighting domestic violence charges, left behind a detailed 24-page suicide note, explaining the challenges he had been facing. The note mentioned multiple police complaints filed against him by his wife and others, which he claimed had pushed him to take the extreme step, a TOI report stated.

Atul sent a detailed Email to NGO

The incident was first brought to light when Atul sent an email late Sunday night to a non-governmental organisation (NGO), advocating for men suffering from domestic violence. The email revealed Atul's intention to end his life, prompting the NGO staff to alert the police. With the information provided by the NGO, police arrived at his apartment, broke down the door, and discovered his body.

Death Note and Chilling Instructions Found

Upon discovering Atul's body, the police found a chilling message. An A4 sheet glued to his chest read, "Justice is Due." Police discovered a detailed timetable and instructions written in English and Hindi. These outlined his actions before his death and instructions for afterward. The timetable included tasks such as prayer, organizing belongings, and emailing his workplace and courts.

47

The New Indian Express

https://www.newindianexpress.com/cities/bengaluru/2024/Dec/10/techie-ends-life-over-harassment-blames-wife-her-kin-in-suicide-note

Bengaluru

Techie ends life over 'harassment', blames wife, her kin in suicide note

He also described the burden of the nine cases filed against him and his parents, which forced him to frequently travel between Bengaluru and Jaunpur.

Representative Image File Photo

Express News Service

Updated on: 10 Dec 2024, 9:05 am · 2 min read

BENGALURU: A 34-year-old software engineer died by suicide at his residence in Marathahalli, leaving a 24-page death note behind. He had stuck a sheet of paper printed with 'Justice is Due' on the T-shirt he was wearing. It is suspected that the man took the extreme step due to alleged harassment by his wife and her family. He also recorded a video before hanging himself in his room. The deceased Atul Subhash was from Uttar Pradesh.

The police said Subhash was reportedly suffering from depression. Before taking the extreme step, Subhash sent a message at midnight on the WhatsApp group of an NGO which deals with domestic harassment by women, informing that he was ending his life.

A group member saw the message in the morning and alerted police, who reached his room to find him hanging, with a sheet of paper pasted on his T-shirt that read 'Justice is Due'. He had also pasted printouts on the wall with the same message.

Related Stories

Winter session of Odisha Assembly starts on a stormy note

Express News Service ·
26 Nov 2024

11-page suicide note of the Karnataka Bhovi Corporation scam accused is sent to the FSL

Express News Service ·
25 Nov 2024

Two Rajasthani youths held by Mangalore police for cheating Amazon of Rs 1.2 crore

Express News Service ·
04 Nov 2024

Five PWD engineers to be prosecuted for Rs 200 crore scam at hospitals

Express News Service ·
29 Oct 2024

The Logical Indian

https://thelogicalindian.com/the-logical-indian/bengaluru-engineer-atul-subhash-dies-by-suicide-leaves-heartfelt-24-page-note-alleging-harassment-and-crying-for-justice/

Search   Q   Contact

Bengaluru Engineer Atul Subhash Dies by Suicide, Leaves Heartfelt 24-Page Note Alleging Harassment and Crying for Justice

A 34-year-old software engineer's tragic suicide in Bengaluru highlights the devastating impact of domestic disputes and mental health struggles.

 News Desk   December 10, 2024

Atul Subhash, a 34-year-old software engineer from Uttar Pradesh, died by suicide in his Bengaluru home on December 9, 2024, leaving behind a 24-page note that alleged harassment by his estranged wife and her family. The note detailed his emotional distress stemming from multiple legal cases filed against him. Authorities are investigating the incident, with charges of abetment filed against his wife and her relatives following a complaint from Subhash's brother. This tragic case has sparked discussions about the mental health implications of domestic disputes.

Featured

Times of India

https://timesofindia.indiatimes.com/india/rs-3-crore-for-settlement-9-police-cases-bengaluru-techies-brother-alleges-harassment-by-wife-in-laws-in-suicide-case/articleshow/116179499.cms

Hindustan Times

https://www.hindustantimes.com/cities/bengaluru-news/bengaluru-techie-dies-by-suicide-alleges-harassment-by-wife-in-24-page-death-note-101733804887999.html

MoneyControl

https://www.moneycontrol.com/news/india/bengaluru-suicide-techie-commits-suicide-in-bengaluru-blames-wife-in-24-page-note-12886432.html

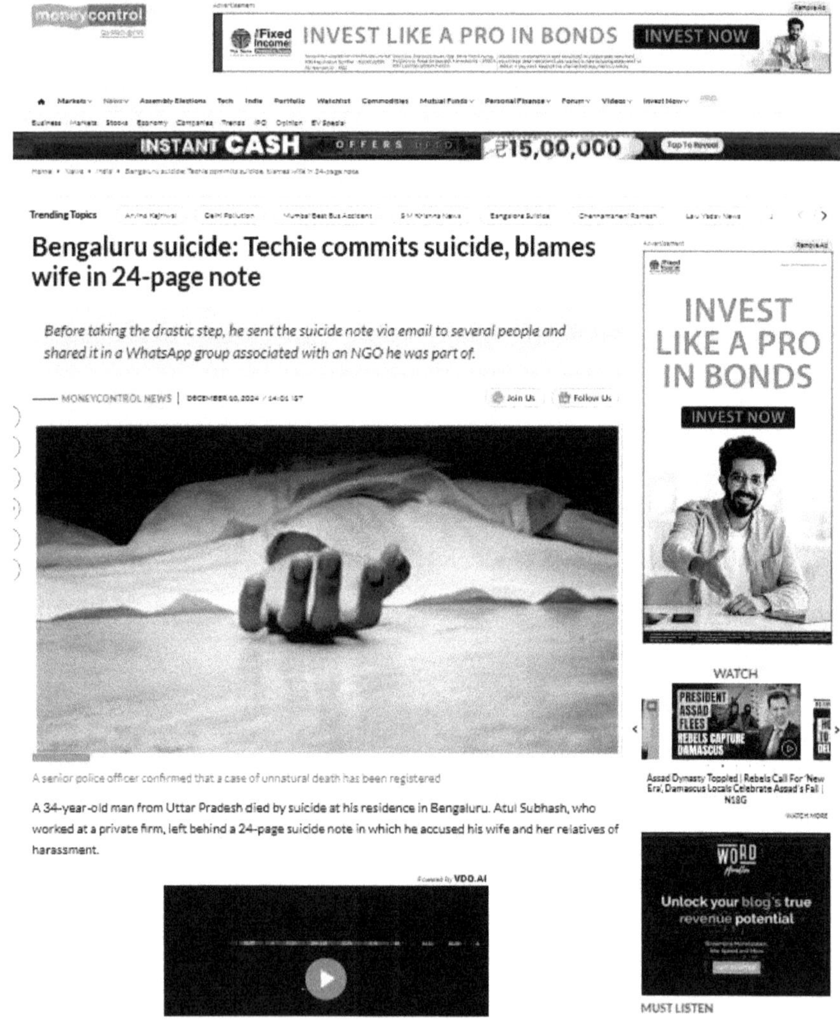

News18

https://www.news18.com/viral/justice-is-due-up-man-dies-by-suicide-in-bengaluru-leaves-behind-24-page-note-9151033.html

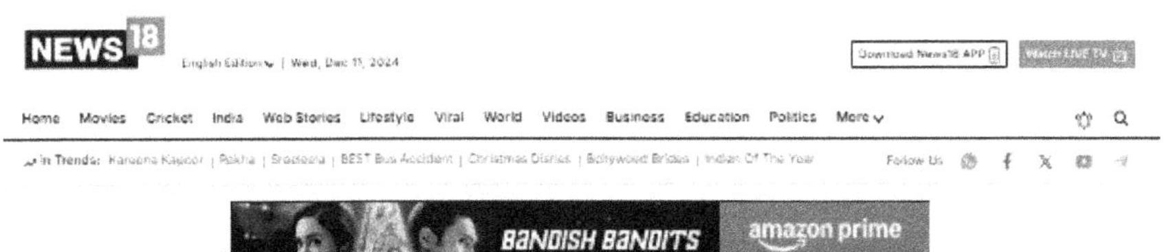

'Justice Is Due': Engineer Dies By Suicide In Bengaluru, Leaves Behind 24-Page Note

Curated By: Arfa Javaid News18.com

Last Updated: December 10, 2024, 15:13 IST

Before taking the drastic step, the Bengaluru engineer sent the suicide note via email to several people and shared it in a WhatsApp group associated with an NGO he was part of.

Initial investigations suggest that defendants showed anger over Atul Subhash had been facing marital issues

A 34-year-old man from Uttar Pradesh died by suicide at his residence in Bengaluru on Monday. Atul Subhash, who was an engineer at a private firm, left behind a 24-page suicide note in which he accused his wife and her relatives of harassment.

Initial investigations suggest that Subhash had been facing marital issues, and his wife had filed several cases against him in Uttar Pradesh which he discussed at length in a video. Before taking the drastic step, he sent the suicide note via email to several people and shared it in a WhatsApp group associated with an NGO he was part of.

'Crime To Be A Man In India': #MenToo Trends As Netizens Seek Justice For Atul Subhash

MORE IMPACT SHORTS

RELATED STORIES

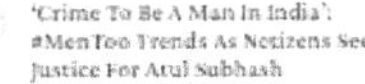

'Crime To Be A Man In India': #MenToo Trends As Netizens Seek Justice For Atul Subhash

'Child's Custody To Grandparents, His Ashes Shouldn't Be Immersed Until...':...

'A Dead Man Is Requesting...': Bengaluru Engineer's Last Post Was Big Appeal To Trump, Musk

Bengaluru Techie Suicide: Case Registered As Netizens Call For Justice

Subhash also recorded a video and shared it on social media before taking the drastic step. Alongside, he wrote, "...A legal genocide of men happening in India currently."

According to the police, Subhash hung a placard in his house that read "Justice is due".

Before taking the extreme step, he allegedly pasted important details on a cupboard, including information about his 24-page suicide note, vehicle keys, and a list of tasks he had completed and those still pending.

LATEST NEWS

Latest Entertainment News Live Updates Today (December 10, 2024): Sunny Deol...

Sunny Deol Makes Shocking Revelation, Says Big Production Houses Didn't Want To...

Bihar Man Travels To US On Andhra Girl's Advice, Secures Job With Rs 2.5 Crore Package

Meghan Markle Once Turned Down Ex-ESPN Host Who Believed She Was 'Obtainable'

Meet Anurag Kashyap's Soon-To-Be Son-In-Law

India Today

https://www.indiatoday.in/cities/bengaluru/story/bengaluru-techie-atul-subhash-brother-on-suicide-harassment-by-wife-in-laws-2647786-2024-12-10

NewsX

https://www.newsx.com/india/justice-for-atul-subhash-trending-ends-life-blaming-wife-watch-his-last-video/

HOME » India » Justice For Atul Subhash Trending? Ends Life Blaming Wife, WATCH His Last Video

Justice For Atul Subhash Trending? Ends Life Blaming Wife, WATCH His Last Video

A tragic case of Bengaluru-based tech entrepreneur Atul Subhash, has led to broad outrage across social media forums.

By Swastika Shut
December 10, 2024 1:59 pm Asia/Kolkata IST; Updated 10 hours ago

A tragic case of Bengaluru-based tech entrepreneur Atul Subhash, has led to broad outrage across social media forums. Through a shocking post published to X (formerly Twitter), Atul wrote, "A legal genocide of men is happening in India." He had tagged major world leaders like US President Donald Trump and Tesla head Elon Musk along with many other prominent public personalities and global leaders in the now-deleted post.

His haunting words, "I will be dead when you will read this," have left netizens demanding accountability and justice.

Zee News

https://zeenews.india.com/technology/casualty-of-system-techie-atul-subhash-dies-by-suicide-after-years-of-harassment-by-wife-family-court-netizens-react-2830041.html

Casualty Of System? Techie Atul Subhash Dies By Suicide After Years Of 'Harassment' By Wife, Family Court; Netizens React

Bengaluru Techie Suicide Case: According to early investigations, Atul had been facing problems in his marriage, and his wife had filed a case against him in Uttar Pradesh.

Written By Zee Media Bureau | Edited By: Ankur Mishra | Last Updated: Dec 10, 2024, 06:58 PM IST | Source: Bureau

Trending Photos

Swankier, Luxurious: Indian Railways Unveils First Look of Vande Bharat Sleeper Train Prototype; Check PICS

From Cheteshwar Pujara To Ajinkya Rahane, 6 Players From India's Epic Gabba Win In 2021 Who Won't Be Part Of Playing XI This Time

Your Aadhaar At Risk Of Being Misused By Hackers? Keep It Safe Using Masked Aadhaar

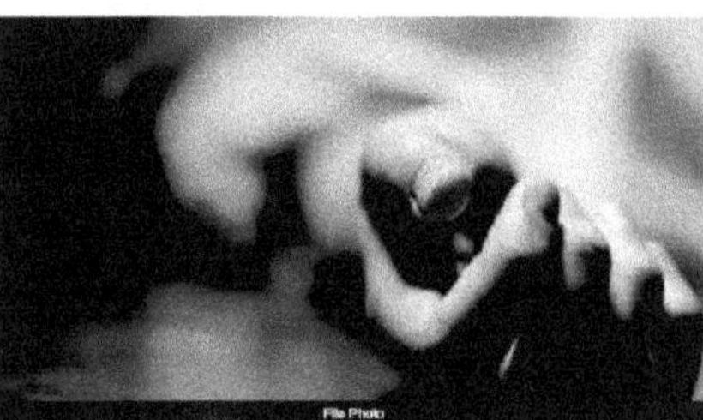

File Photo

Bengaluru Techie Suicide Case: Atul Subhash, a 34-year-old engineer from Jaunpur, Uttar Pradesh, who worked at a private company in Bengaluru, tragically took his own life. His body was found in Marathahalli, Bengaluru, where he had hung himself. Police discovered a 24-page death note in which he accused his wife and her family of harassing him. However, the police have launched an in-depth investigation into the circumstances surrounding his death.

End Of Year Sale

Ethos Watch Boutiques

According to early investigations, Atul had been facing problems in his

Live Tv

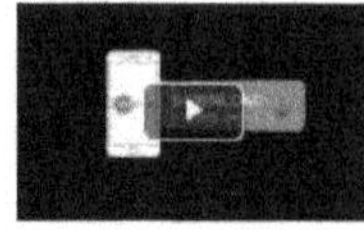

Trending news

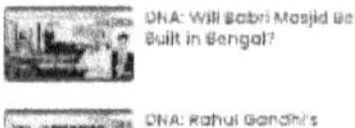

DNA: Fake Milk Factory Busted In Bulandshahr

DNA: Will Babri Masjid Be Built In Bengal?

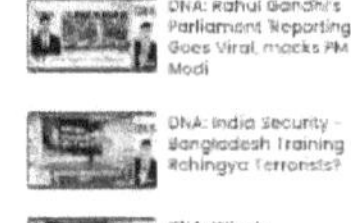

DNA: Rahul Gandhi's 'Parliament Reporting' Goes Viral, mocks PM Modi

DNA: India Security - Bangladesh Training Rohingya Terrorists?

DNA: Why Is 'Mohammad' the Most

Business Today

https://www.businesstoday.in/india/story/bengaluru-techie-ends-life-by-suicide-leaves-24-page-note-accusing-estranged-wife-and-family-of-harassment-456822-2024-12-10

Subhash, employed at a private firm, detailed his struggles in the note, which consisted of four handwritten pages and 20 typed ones.

A 34-year-old software engineer from Uttar Pradesh, working in Bengaluru, died by suicide at his residence in Manjunath Layout. The man, identified as Atul Subhash, left behind a 24-page note accusing his estranged wife and her family of harassment, as revealed by the police.

Subhash, employed at a private firm, detailed his struggles in the note, which consisted of four handwritten pages and 20 typed ones. He began the note with the words, **"Justice is Due"**, and alleged harassment by his wife, her mother, brother, and uncle, attributing his decision to ongoing marital discord. Subhash also 'symbolically' mentioned his four-year-old son, describing him as 'innocent' but alleging he was being used as a tool to demand maintenance.

ABP Live

https://news.abplive.com/cities/bengaluru-techie-suicide-sparks-justice-for-atul-subhash-trend-on-x-twitter-social-media-reactions-divided-1736871

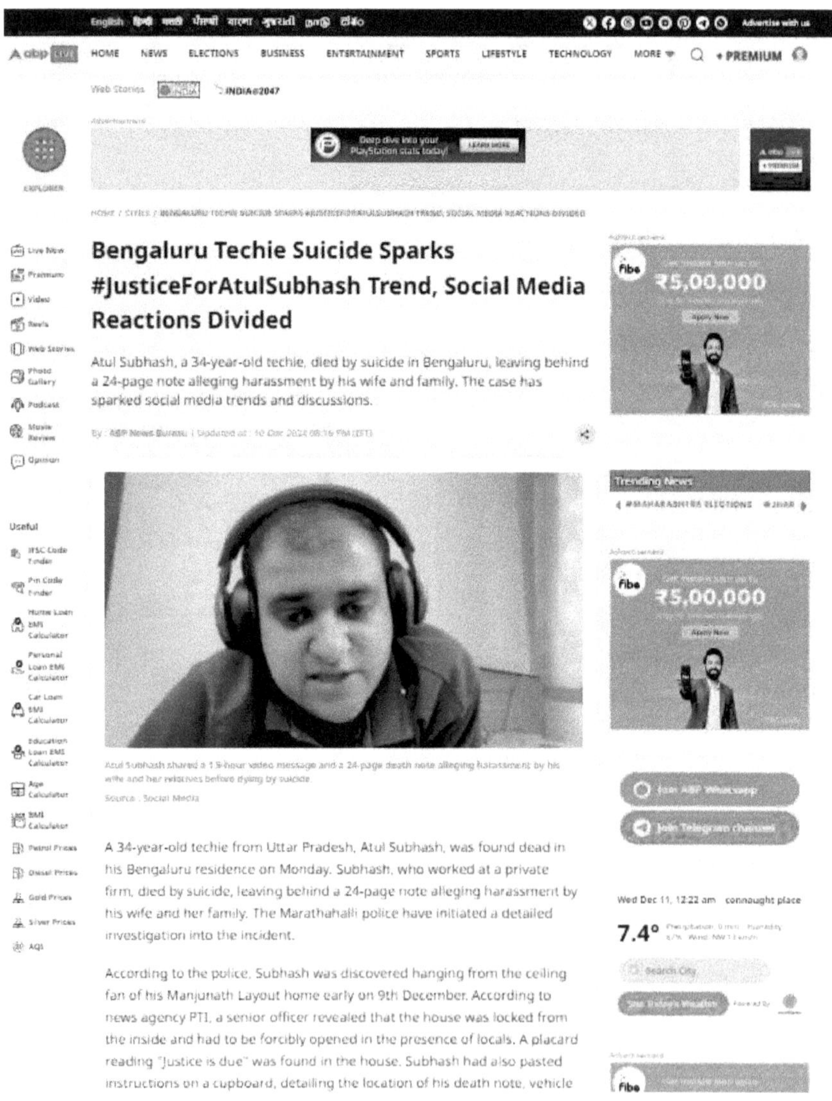

Bengaluru Techie Suicide Sparks #JusticeForAtulSubhash Trend, Social Media Reactions Divided

Atul Subhash, a 34-year-old techie, died by suicide in Bengaluru, leaving behind a 24-page note alleging harassment by his wife and family. The case has sparked social media trends and discussions.

By : ABP News Bureau | Updated at : 10 Dec 2024 08:16 PM (IST)

Atul Subhash shared a 1.5-hour video message and a 24-page death note alleging harassment by his wife and her relatives before dying by suicide.

Source : Social Media

A 34-year-old techie from Uttar Pradesh, Atul Subhash, was found dead in his Bengaluru residence on Monday. Subhash, who worked at a private firm, died by suicide, leaving behind a 24-page note alleging harassment by his wife and her family. The Marathahalli police have initiated a detailed investigation into the incident.

According to the police, Subhash was discovered hanging from the ceiling fan of his Manjunath Layout home early on 9th December. According to news agency PTI, a senior officer revealed that the house was locked from the inside and had to be forcibly opened in the presence of locals. A placard reading "Justice is due" was found in the house. Subhash had also pasted instructions on a cupboard, detailing the location of his death note, vehicle

Times Now

https://www.timesnownews.com/bengaluru/bengaluru-techie-suicide-atul-subhash-viral-video-unnatural-sex-charge-wife-harassment-article-116169445

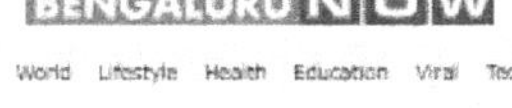

News / Bengaluru News

Bengaluru Techie's Final Video Before Suicide Goes Viral: 'Unnatural Sex Charge, Rs 3 Crore Demand By Wife'

34-year-old Atul Subhash, who worked at a private firm in Bengaluru, was found hanging at his residence in the city's Manjunath Layout area in Bengaluru. Before taking the extreme step, Atul recorded a 84-minute video and left behind a 24-page suicide note accusing wife of harassment.

Edited by: Priya Pareek | Updated Dec 10, 2024, 15:58 IST

Representative image

Related News >>

Zero Fatalities in 3 Months: How Bengaluru-Mysuru Highway's...

How Newly Opened Karnataka Section Of...

How SM Krishna Played A Key Role In Putting...

'Justice Is Due!': UP Man Dies By Suicide In...

Misty Conditions Likely In Bengaluru Today; On-And-...

Bengaluru: A 34-year-old techie from Uttar Pradesh died by suicide at his Bengaluru residence and left behind a 24-page note and a video recording in which he accused his estranged wife and her family of harassment. In the video, the techie, Atul Subhash, detailed how harassment by his wife pushed him to take the extreme step.

According to the police, 34-year-old Atul Subhash, who worked at a private firm in Bengaluru, was found hanging at his residence in the city's Manjunath Layout area. He left an 84-minute video explaining everything and a part of the clip is being widely shared on social media.

Atul began the video by introducing himself, "Hello world, my name is Atul Subhash. I am almost 34 years old. I live in Bangalore. Today, I am going to commit suicide. I believe that it is best for me to kill myself. Because I am making my enemy stronger with the money I am earning. The same money is being used to destroy me. And this cycle will continue to increase."

He added, "With my taxes, this court, this police system, will harass me and my family and other good people as well. So, we should end the supply of value. And anyway, they gave me a suggestion. They told me to commit suicide. And I think they are right. That's the right solution, what they have suggested me. So, I am going to kill myself."

He added, "My wife and her family should not come near me. Thirdly, my identity should not be revealed until my harassers get punished. So, my identity should not be revealed. Even after all these things, evidence, and everything, if the court does not punish the judge and my other harassers, and releases them, then my identity should be thrown out of the court in a gutter. So that I know that I should continue to learn my lesson that what is the value of a life in this country. So, this is one thing. And I will talk to my parents and brothers separately. If possible, forgive me. At the age when I had to support my parents, at that age, I am hurting them forever."

ANI

https://www.aninews.in/news/national/general-news/karnataka-techie-dies-by-suicide-leaves-24-page-death-note-accusing-wife-her-family-members20241210173559/

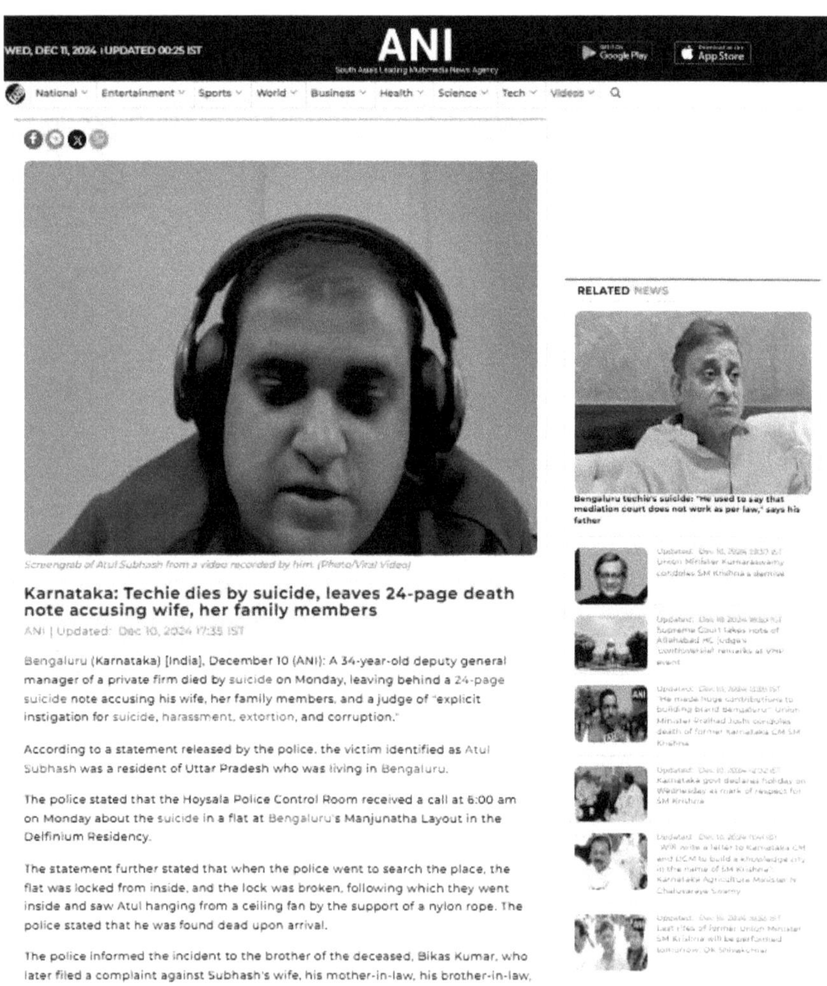

Screengrab of Atul Subhash from a video recorded by him. (Photo/Viral Video)

Karnataka: Techie dies by suicide, leaves 24-page death note accusing wife, her family members

ANI | Updated: Dec 10, 2024 17:35 IST

Bengaluru (Karnataka) [India], December 10 (ANI): A 34-year-old deputy general manager of a private firm died by suicide on Monday, leaving behind a 24-page suicide note accusing his wife, her family members, and a judge of "explicit instigation for suicide, harassment, extortion, and corruption."

According to a statement released by the police, the victim identified as Atul Subhash was a resident of Uttar Pradesh who was living in Bengaluru.

The police stated that the Hoysala Police Control Room received a call at 6:00 am on Monday about the suicide in a flat at Bengaluru's Manjunatha Layout in the Delfinium Residency.

The statement further stated that when the police went to search the place, the flat was locked from inside, and the lock was broken, following which they went inside and saw Atul hanging from a ceiling fan by the support of a nylon rope. The police stated that he was found dead upon arrival.

The police informed the incident to the brother of the deceased, Bikas Kumar, who later filed a complaint against Subhash's wife, his mother-in-law, his brother-in-law, and his wife's uncle, accusing them of filing a false complaint against Subhash and demanding Rs 3 crore money for the settlement, which led to his mental and physical harassment, following which he had to take the step.

The Week

https://www.theweek.in/news/india/2024/12/10/why-did-atul-subhash-kill-himself-chilling-24-page-suicide-note-by-bengaluru-techie-blames-estranged-wife.html

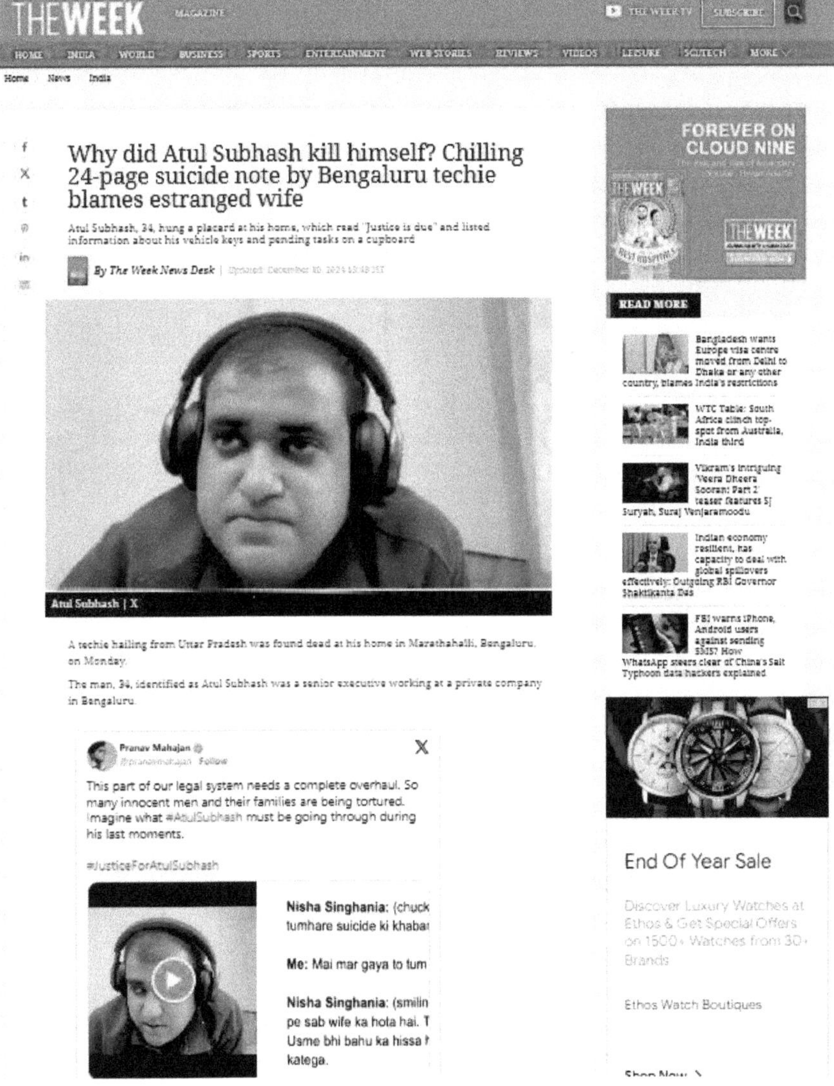

61

The Hindu

https://www.thehindu.com/news/national/karnataka/private-firm-senior-executive-ends-life-in-bengalurus-marathahalli-probe-on/article68966249.ece

Private firm senior executive ends life in Bengaluru's Marathahalli; probe on

The police have registered a case of unnatural death, charging his wife and her relatives for abetment

Updated : December 10, 2024 07:16 pm IST - Bengaluru

THE HINDU BUREAU

READ LATER   PRINT

A 34-year-old senior executive of a private company allegedly died by suicide at his apartment in Munekolala in Marathahalli on Monday.

Launching Capstone Properties

Capstone Properties   Open >

ADVERTISEMENT

Most Popular

Bangalore Mirror

https://bangaloremirror.indiatimes.com/bangalore/crime/man-dies-by-suicide-leaves-40-page-death-note/articleshow/116147381.cms

Man dies by suicide, leaves 40-page death note

IANS / Updated: Dec 10, 2024, 06:00 IST

A man died by suicide at his home in an upscale locality of Manjunatha Layout, the police said on Monday, adding that he also left behind an over 40-page suicide note.

According to the police, the deceased has been identified as Atul Subhash, who hails from Uttar Pradesh. An initial investigation by the police revealed that Atul Subhash's wife had filed a case against him in Uttar Pradesh.

It is being suspected that he ended his life due to marital discord. Atul was a member of the "Save Indian Family Foundation," an NGO that provides 'assistance to victims of false cases filed by spouses'.

The police said that he had also created a "time-table" for two days to commit suicide.

In his suicide note, Atul outlined specific actions to be taken before dying under three headings. The first heading read, "what should be done before dying", in which he wrote: "Take a bath, open the windows and gate lock, recite the name of Lord Shiva 100 times, keep the keys of the car and bike on the fridge, and place the note on the table."

He also mentioned that "the suicide note should be sent to the High Court, Supreme Court, office, and family". He concluded by writing, "one should destroy self".

In the second heading, "what should be done one day earlier", Atul 'suggested' clearing all financial matters, completing all communication and office work, and finalising legal issues. He suggested packing essential documents and preparing for the final day.

In the third section, titled "the final day", Atul said on that very day, a 'video note' should be uploaded. He mentioned erasing fingerprints and face recognition data from mobile phones, returning the laptop, charger, and ID to the office, and uploading a scanned copy of the 'death note'. He mentioned ensuring all payments were completed before taking the final step.

Dainik Jagaran

https://english.jagran.com/india/atul-subhash-suicide-bengaluru-techie-news-suicide-note-harassment-by-wife-maintenance-demand-children-custody-viral-video-10206070

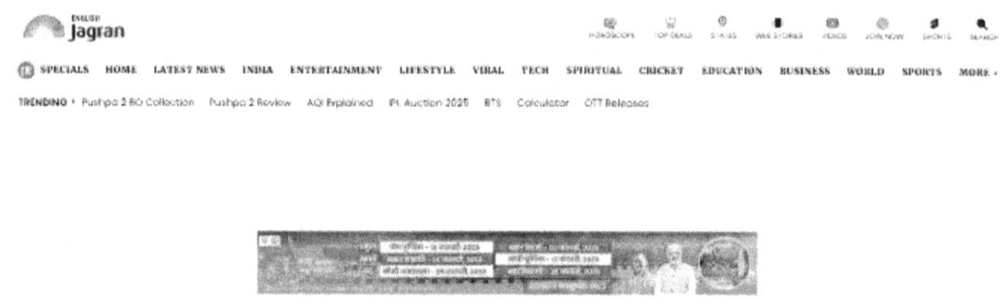

Bengaluru Engineer Dies By Suicide, Alleges Harassment By Wife In 24-Page Note, Last Video Goes Viral | Watch

Atul Subhash Death: The incident occurred in the Manjunath Layout area, which falls under the Marathahalli police station limits. According to the preliminary probe, Subhash had been facing marital discord with his wife, and she had registered a case against him in Uttar Pradesh.

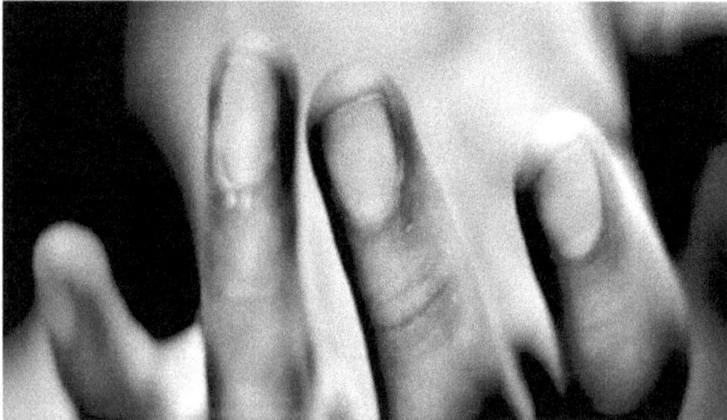

Atul Subhash Suicide: A video has gone viral on social media of Atul where he could be heard explaining everything. (Image used for representation.)

About Save Indian Family Foundation

Save Indian Family Foundation (SIFF) is a non-funded non-profit NGO fighting for men's rights, Gender Equality and Family Harmony by creating awareness against gender biased laws like 498a and Domestic Violence (DV) Act in India. It fights for men's human rights and seeks to protect men and their families from government sponsored undemocratic social experiments. The primary goal of SIFF is to put an end to the epidemic of false dowry, false domestic violence and false rape cases in India, to create gender neutral laws and end discrimination of men and male disposability.

SIFF's Mission is to expose and create awareness about large scale violations of Civil Liberties and Human Rights in the name of women's empowerment in India. SIFF works for ending Male Disposability in India and the world. Most of the common men are so much brainwashed by the society that they fail to see that Males are Disposable Gender and deaths of men often does not count for the societies across the world. For example, 3 times more men than women die in accidents, murders and suicides in India. Yet, this is not considered when people talk about gender equality. SIFF also supports male victims of domestic violence and false dowry cases. SIFF wants all the laws in India to be made gender neutral.

SIFF provides guidance and support to men and their families, who face domestic violence and false cases of dowry harassment and section 498a. SIFF protects these men and families from extortion by a corrupt police and court system, where laws are used to coerce men to cough up huge sums of money as out of court settlement, with complete disregard to basic principles of law and natural justice. SIFF works to prevent suicides of men, who are victims of domestic violence and false cases filed by wives. SIFF also campaigns for gender neutral laws and ending of misuse of all laws. SIFF often helps men get in touch with their inner selves and their emotions, so that these men can get peace, when they have marital problems.

The website of SIFF is https://www.saveindianfamily.org

Other Books by Save Indian Family Foundation

We the Men of India: A Collection of Writings